REPRO QUILTS

by Christiane Meunier and the Moon Over Mountain Quilters

Moon over Mountain

2 Public Avenue,
Montrose, PA 18801-1220
www.QuiltTownUSA.com

About the
Moon over Mountain Quilters

Moon Over Mountain
2 Public Avenue
Montrose, Pennsylvania 18801-1220

First Printing: 2005

Library of Congress Cataloging-in-Publication Data
Repro-quilts : quilts made using reproduction fabrics / by Christiane Meunier and more.
   p. cm.
ISBN 1-885588-70-4 (pbk.)
   1. Strip quilting—Patterns. 2. Patchwork—Patterns.
   3. Quilting—Patterns. I. Meunier, Christiane.
TT835.R4564 2006
746.46'041—dc22

2005027128

Design and Illustrations..Diane Albeck-Grick
Photography....................Van Zandbergen Photography,
Brackney, Pennsylvania

Our Mission Statement
We publish quality quilting books that recognize, promote, and inspire self-expression. We are dedicated to serving our customers with respect, kindness, and efficiency.

www.QuiltTownUSA.com

The Moon Over Mountain Quilters are a nationwide community of quilters dedicated to honoring our heritage by keeping the tradition of quilting alive. They make quilts of astonishing beauty which are deeply rooted in tradition using the large variety of fabrics and tools available to today's quilters. In keeping with our foremothers' tradition of generosity, they are happy to share their know-how and their patterns with fellow quilters.

Christiane Meunier, author of 14 popular quilting books, has been a leader in the quilt world since publishing Quilting Today magazine in 1987. She has also earned acclaim as a quilt designer whose works have been featured in numerous publications and shows. Christiane's incredible sense of color guides her to create quilts that speak to all who view them.

by Debra Feece **8**

by Sue De Salvatore **10**

12 *by Kathy Delaney*

16 *by Kathy Rapley*

by Judy Forsey **22**

by Denice Lipscomb **24**

26 *by Denice Lipscomb*

Blazing Stars

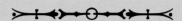

Materials

- Assorted light, medium and dark print fabrics in 1 7/8" x 30" strips and totaling 9 yards
- 7 1/4 yards beige
- 3/4 yard brown for the piping
- 8 yards backing fabric
- 97" square of batting
- 10 1/2 yards 1/8" cording for the piping

Cutting

Pattern piece A (page 7) is full size and includes a 1/4" seam allowance, as do all dimensions given. Cut the lengthwise beige strips before cutting other pieces from that fabric.
NOTE: *Choose 4 or 5 prints for each block. Designate a light, medium or dark print for the center of the Star (label it fabric #1) and medium or dark print for the tips of the Star points (label it fabric #5). Label the other prints #2, #3, and #4, in the order you want them to appear from the center to the points.*

For each Star block:
- Cut 1: 1 7/8" x 30" strip, fabric #1
- Cut 2: 1 7/8" x 30" strips, fabric #2
- Cut 3: 1 7/8" x 30" strips, fabric #3
- Cut 2: 1 7/8" x 30" strips, fabric #4
- Cut 1: 1 7/8" x 30" strip, fabric #5

For the pieced border:
- Cut 24: 1 7/8" x 30" strips, assorted light, medium, and dark print fabrics

Also:
- Cut 4: 2 1/4" x 95" lengthwise strips, beige, for the outer border
- Cut 4: 2 1/4" x 85" lengthwise strips, beige, for the inner border
- Cut 64: 6 3/4" squares, beige
- Cut 16: 10" squares, beige, then cut them in quarters diagonally to yield 64 triangles
- Cut 104: A, beige
- Cut 10: 2 1/2" x 40" strips, beige, for the binding
- Cut 7/8"-wide bias strips, brown, to total at least 375" when joined for the piping

Directions

For each Star block:

1. Lay out one 1 7/8" x 30" strip each of fabrics #1, #2, and #3, in order from bottom to top. Sew them together along their length to make a pieced panel. Trim the left end of the pieced panel at a 45° angle, as shown.

2. Measuring from the trimmed edge, cut a 1 7/8" section from the pieced panel. In the same manner, cut 7 more 1 7/8" sections from the panel. Label them Row A and set them aside.

3. Lay out one 1 7/8" x 30" strip each of fabrics #2, #3, and #4, in order from bottom to top. Sew them together to make a pieced panel.

4. Trim the left end of the pieced panel at a 45° angle, as before. Cut eight 1 7/8" sections from the pieced panel. Label them Row B and set them aside.

5. Lay out one 1 7/8" x 30" strip each of fabrics #3, #4, and #5, in order from bottom to top. Sew them together to make a pieced panel.

6. Trim the left end of the pieced panel. Cut eight 1 7/8" sections from the pieced panel. Label them Row C.

7. Lay out one each of Rows A, B, and C. Sew them together to make a Star Point, as shown. Make 8.

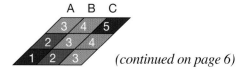

(continued on page 6)

4

*Gayle Hawley of Independence, Missouri, originally made **"Blazing Stars"** as a friendship project with members of her guild. Gayle assembled the top after friends helped make sections of the stars. She then hand quilted this beauty and added machine trapunto. Gayle says she enjoys all kinds of quilts but likes traditional designs best. Her favorite part of making a quilt is the quilting.*

(continued from page 4)

8. Join 2 Star Points to make a quarter-star, keeping the #1 fabric diamonds together, and carefully matching the seams. Start and stop stitching at the 1/4" seamlines and backstitch. Make 4.

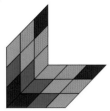

9. In the same manner, join 2 quarter-stars to make a half-star. Make 2. Sew the 2 half-stars together to make a Star.

10. Set 4 beige triangles and four 6 3/4" beige squares into the Star, as shown. NOTE: *The squares and triangles are slightly oversized to allow for trimming the finished block. Make 16.*

11. Square each block by trimming the edges 1/4" beyond the tips of the Star points.

For the border diamonds:

1. Sew 2 contrasting 1 7/8" x 30" print strips together along their length to make a pieced strip. Make 12.

2. Trim the left end of a pieced strip at a 45° angle, as before. Cut 8 more 1 7/8" sections from the pieced strip.

3. In the same manner, cut eight 1 7/8" sections from each remaining pieced strip.

4. Join 2 matching sections to make a border diamond. Make 48.

Assembly

1. Lay out the blocks in 4 rows of 4. Sew the blocks into rows and join the rows.

2. Lay out 12 border diamonds and 26 beige A's, as shown. Join them to make a pieced border. Make 4.

3. Fold a 2 1/4" x 85" beige print strip in half and finger press the fold to mark the center. Measure 39 1/8" from the center and make a mark on the 1/4" seamline at that point. Make a mark 39 1/8" from the center in the opposite direction. Mark the remaining 2 1/4" x 85" beige print strips in the same manner.

4. Pin a marked beige print strip to a pieced border, matching their centers and aligning the marks on the strip with the side points of the end border diamonds. Sew the strip to the pieced border. Sew one of the remaining 2 1/4" x 85" beige print strips to each of the remaining pieced borders in the same manner.

5. Pin a 2 1/4" x 95" beige print strip to the remaining side of a pieced border, matching their centers. Sew the strip to the border. Make 4.

6. Lay out one border. Measure 39 3/4" from the center of the shorter beige print strip and make a mark on the 1/4" seamline at that point. Make a mark 39 3/4" from the center in the opposite direction. Mark the remaining borders in the same manner.

7. Center and pin a border to one side of the quilt, aligning the marks on the strips with the 1/4" seamlines of the quilt. Sew the border to the quilt between the marks, backstitching at each mark to secure the seam. Sew the remaining borders to the quilt in the same manner.

8. Miter the corners, referring to the *General Directions* as necessary.

For the Piping:

1. Place the 1/8" cording on the wrong side of the 7/8"-wide brown bias strip. Fold the bias strip in half, right side out, aligning the raw edges and enclosing the cording along the fold. Using a zipper foot, stitch close to the cording.

2. Aligning the raw edges, lay the piping on the quilt top, starting 6" or 7" from one corner and about 2" from the end of the piping. Using the zipper foot, machine baste the piping to the quilt top, continuing to align the raw edges as you sew. Stop stitching about 1" from the corner.

3. Maneuver the piping to form a right angle at the corner, keeping the raw edges aligned. Clip the seam allowance of the piping to enable it to turn the corner. With the needle down, pivot at the 1/4" seamline and continue basting the piping to the quilt, as before.

4. Continue stitching to about 4" from the starting point and remove the quilt top from the machine.

5. Lay the ends of the piping on the quilt top and mark them at the point where they meet. Trim the ends 1/4" beyond the marks.

6. Remove 1" of the piping stitches from each end. Open the piping and trim 1/4" from each end of the cording.

7. Stitch the ends of the bias strip together, using a 1/4" seam. Finger press the seam open.

8. Refold the bias strip, enclosing the ends of the cording. Align the raw edges and finish basting the piping to the quilt top.

9. Finish the quilt according to the *General Directions*, using the 2 1/2" x 40" beige strips for the binding.

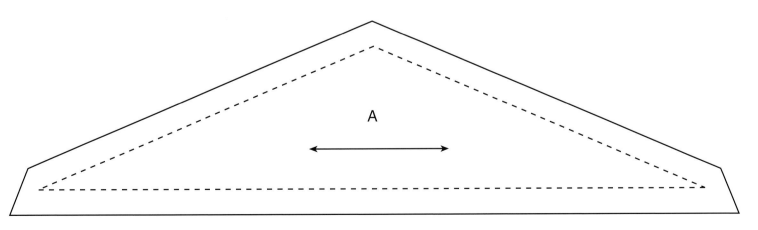

A

Churn Dash

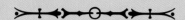

Materials

- Assorted blue prints,
  totaling at least 4 yards
- Assorted shirting prints,
  totaling at least 4 1/4 yards
- 1 yard blue plaid for the binding
- 8 yards backing fabric
- 84" x 94" piece of batting

Cutting

Dimensions include a 1/4" seam allowance.

NOTE: *For fun and interest, mix up the fabrics in some of your blocks. Debra used just 2 fabrics for some blocks and 3, 4, or more for others.*

For each of 72 blocks:

- Cut 2: 4 7/8" squares, one blue print
- Cut 4: 2 1/2" squares, same blue print
- Cut 2: 4 7/8" squares, one shirting print
- Cut 5: 2 1/2" squares, same shirting print

Also:

- Cut 2 1/2"-wide bias strips, blue plaid, to total 355" when joined for the binding

Directions

For each block:

1. Draw a diagonal line from corner to corner on the wrong side of the 4 7/8" shirting print squares.

2. Place a marked square on a 4 7/8" blue print square, right sides together. Sew 1/4" away from the drawn line on both sides. Make 2.

3. Cut the squares on the drawn lines to yield 4 pieced squares. Press the seam allowances toward the blue print.

4. Sew a 2 1/2" shirting print square to a 2 1/2" blue print square to make a pieced rectangle. Make 4. Press the seam allowances toward the blue print.

5. Lay out the pieced squares, pieced rectangles, and remaining 2 1/2" shirting print square. Sew the units into rows and join the rows to complete the block. Make 72.

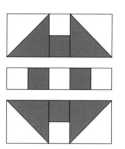

Assembly

1. Lay out the blocks in 9 rows of 8. Sew the blocks into rows and join the rows.

2. Finish the quilt as described in the *General Directions*, using the 2 1/2"-wide blue plaid bias strips for the binding.

ALTERNATE SIZE CHART FOR CHURN DASH		
Quilt Size	**Throw (60" sq.)**	**Twin (70" x 80")**
No. of blocks	36 (6 x 6)	56 (7 x 8)
Blue prints	at least 2 1/8 yards	at least 3 1/4 yards
Shirting prints	at least 2 1/4 yards	at least 3 1/2 yards
Backing	3 3/4 yards	4 3/4 yards
Batting	64" square	74" x 84"

Debra Feece collected blue prints and shirtings for over a year with a **Churn Dash** quilt in mind. Knowing only that she wanted to make that block but unsure of the layout—did she want sashing or borders, blocks on point or straight—she kept buying fabric! Then an antique quilt inspired Debra and answered all of those design questions. Debra loves the simplicity of old utility quilts and she knew right away she wanted to replicate that quilt.

Prairie Sunrise

Materials

- Assorted dark prints, each at least 5" x 7 1/2" and totaling at least 2 yards
- Assorted light prints, each at least 3" square and totaling at least 1 yard
- 1/2 yard dark print for the binding
- 3 yards backing fabric
- 52" square of batting

Cutting

Dimensions include a 1/4" seam allowance.

- Cut 72: 4 7/8" squares, assorted dark prints, then cut them in half diagonally to yield 144 triangles
- Cut 2: 2 1/2" squares from each of the same dark prints
- Cut 144: 2 7/8" squares, assorted light prints, then cut them in half diagonally to yield 288 triangles
- Cut 6: 2 1/2" x 40" strips, dark print, for the binding

Directions

1. Sew 2 matching light triangles to a 2 1/2" dark print square. Press the seam allowances toward the triangles.

2. Sew a matching dark print triangle to the unit to make a pieced square. Press the seam allowance toward the triangle. Make 144.

3. Lay out 4 pieced squares and join them to make a block. Make 36.

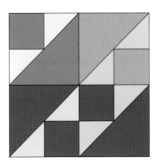

Assembly

1. Referring to the photo, lay out the blocks in 6 rows.
2. Sew the blocks into rows and join the rows.
3. Finish the quilt as described in the *General Directions*, using the 2 1/2" x 40" dark print strips for the binding.

ALTERNATE SIZE CHART FOR PRAIRIE SUNRISE		
Quilt Size	Twin (64" x 72")	Full (72" x 80")
No. of blocks	72 (8 x 9)	90 (9 x 10)
Med. & Dark prints	at least 4 yards	at least 5 yards
Light prints	at least 2 1/8 yards	at least 2 1/2 yards
Backing	4 yards	4 1/2 yards
Batting	68" x 76"	76" x 84"

*Sue De Salvatore of Bandon-by-the-Sea, Oregon, used the popular Dove in Flight block to showcase reproduction fabrics. The warm colors with heavenly blue highlights prompted her to name the quilt "**Prairie Sunrise.**"*

Quilting Feeds My Soul

Materials

- 32 prints, each at least 5" x 10"
- 32 solids, each at least 5" square
- 2 3/4 yards off-white
- 5 1/4 yards yellow solid
- 7 1/2 yards backing fabric
- 87" x 105" piece of batting

Cutting

Dimensions include a 1/4" seam allowance. Cut the lengthwise yellow strips before cutting other pieces from that fabric.

For each of 32 blocks:

- Cut 1: 5" square, solid, then cut it in quarters diagonally to yield 4 triangles
- Cut 2: 4 5/8" squares, coordinating print, then cut them in half diagonally to yield 4 triangles

Also:

- Cut 4: 14 3/8" squares, off-white, then cut them in quarters diagonally to yield 16 setting triangles. You will use 14.
- Cut 2: 7 1/2" squares, off-white, then cut them in half diagonally to yield 4 corner triangles.
- Cut 5: 6 5/8" squares, off-white, then cut them in quarters diagonally to yield 20 small sashing triangles. You will use 18.
- Cut 32: 5" squares, off-white, then cut them in quarters diagonally to yield 128 triangles for the blocks
- Cut 128: 2 1/4" x 4 1/4" rectangles, off-white
- Cut 31: 4 1/4" squares, off-white
- Cut 4: 2 1/2" x 100" lengthwise strips, yellow, for the binding

- Cut 2: 5" x 94" lengthwise strips, yellow, for the border
- Cut 2: 5" x 85" lengthwise strips, yellow, for the border
- Cut 80: 4 1/4" x 9 3/4" strips, yellow, for the sashing
- Cut 32: 2 1/4" squares, yellow

Directions

For each block:

1. Sew an off-white triangle to a solid triangle to make a pieced triangle. Sew a coordinating print triangle to the pieced triangle to make a star unit.

2. Sew a 2 1/4" x 4 1/4" off-white rectangle to the bottom edge of the star unit, as shown. Make 4.

3. Place a 2 1/4" yellow square on a pieced unit, aligning the upper right corners. Sew a partial seam to within 1/2" of the bottom right corner of the square, as shown.

4. Press the seam allowance toward the pieced unit.

5. Sew another pieced unit to the top, as shown, stitching to the end of the yellow square. Press, as before.

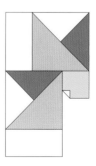

6. Sew a pieced unit to the right side. Sew the remaining
(continued on page 19)

Kathy Delaney of Overland Park, Kansas, says she made every attempt to represent a 1930s quilt with **"Quilting Feeds My Soul."** *Because her grandmother didn't quilt and Kathy wishes she had, she decided to make a quilt that maybe her grandmother would have made. Kathy stitched the traditional Hope of Hartford blocks in a weekend workshop with Liz Porter, then designed her own setting. She researched quilting designs appropriate to the same time period.*

13

Road to Freedom

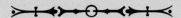

Materials

- **Red and pink print scraps, totaling at least 3/4 yard**
- **Dark print scraps, totaling at least 2 1/2 yards**
- **Light print scraps, totaling at least 2 1/4 yards**
- **3/4 yard light print for the inner border**
- **3/4 yard brown print for the binding**
- **4 3/4 yards backing fabric**
- **67" x 82" piece of batting**

Cutting

All dimensions include a 1/4" seam allowance.

- Cut 96: 3" squares, red and pink prints
- Cut 64: 3" squares, dark prints
- Cut 64: 3 3/8" squares, dark prints
- Cut 16: 8 3/8" squares, dark prints
- Cut 11: 3" x 19" strips, dark prints, for the outer border
- Cut 64: 3 3/8" squares, light prints
- Cut 16: 8 3/8" squares, light prints
- Cut 11: 3" x 19" strips, light prints, for the outer border
- Cut 8: 3" x 40" strips, light print, for the inner border
- Cut 8: 2 1/2" x 40" strips, brown print, for the binding

Directions

1. Draw a diagonal line from corner to corner on the wrong side of each 8 3/8" light print square and each 3 3/8" light print square.

2. Lay a marked 8 3/8" light print square on an 8 3/8" dark print square, right sides together.

3. Sew 1/4" away from the drawn line on both sides. Make 16.

4. Cut the squares on the drawn lines to yield 32 large pieced squares. You will use 31. Press the seam allowances toward the dark print.

5. In the same manner, make pieced squares using the 64 marked 3 3/8" light print squares and the sixty-four 3 3/8" dark print squares. You will have 128 small pieced squares.

6. Lay out three 3" red or pink print squares, two 3" dark print squares and four small pieced squares, as shown. Sew the squares into rows then join the rows to complete a block. Make 32.

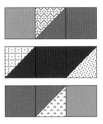

Assembly

1. Referring to the photo, lay out the blocks and large pieced squares in 9 rows of 7.

2. Sew them into rows, then join the rows.

3. Sew the 3" x 40" light print strips together end to end. Cut two 64" lengths and two 80" lengths from the strip. Set them aside.

4. Lay a 3" x 19" dark print strip right side up on a cutting mat. Place a 3" x 19" light print strip, right side up on top of the dark print strip. Make 5 pairs.

5. Using the 45° line on your quilter's ruler, trim the ends of each pair exactly as indicated.

(continued on page 19)

"Road to Freedom," *by Christiane Meunier, has the comfortable understated look of a 19th century scrap quilt. A strong diagonal emphasis was achieved by alternating a variation of the Road to California block with a simple pieced block. For an authentic touch, Christiane included several "intentional errors."*

Log Cabin

Materials

- **3/4 yard each of 8 light prints**
- **1 yard each of 8 dark prints**
- **1 3/4 yards dark red solid**
- **8 yards backing fabric**
- **97" square of batting**

Cutting

Dimensions include a 1/4" seam allowance.

NOTE: *Cut fifteen 1 1/4"-wide strips across the width of each light print and twenty-five 1 1/4"-wide strips from each dark print. Set aside 65 dark print strips for the outer border. Then cut shorter lengths from the remaining strips as indicated.*

From the light print strips:

- Cut 64: 9 1/4" strips
- Cut 64: 8 1/2" strips
- Cut 64: 7 3/4" strips
- Cut 64: 7" strips
- Cut 76: 6 1/4" strips
- Cut 76: 5 1/2" strips
- Cut 76: 4 3/4" strips
- Cut 76: 4" strips
- Cut 76: 3 1/4" strips
- Cut 76: 2 1/2" strips

From the dark print strips:

- Cut 64: 10" strips
- Cut 64: 9 1/4" strips
- Cut 64: 8 1/2" strips
- Cut 64: 7 3/4" strips
- Cut 76: 7" strips
- Cut 76: 6 1/4" strips
- Cut 76: 5 1/2" strips
- Cut 76: 4 3/4" strips
- Cut 76: 4" strips
- Cut 76: 3 1/4" strips

Also:

- Cut 10: 7" strips, assorted dark prints, for the outer border
- Cut 24: 7" strips, assorted light prints, for the outer border
- Cut 76: 2 1/2" squares, dark red solid
- Cut 8: 2" x 40" strips, dark red solid, for the inner border
- Cut 10: 2 1/2" x 40" strips, dark red solid, for the binding

Directions

1. Sew a 2 1/2"-long light print strip to a 2 1/2" dark red solid square. Without lifting the presser foot or cutting the thread, sew another 2 1/2" light print strip to a red square. Chain piece 76 units in this manner.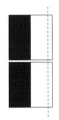

2. Cut the units apart and press the seam allowances toward the strips. Stack them right side up with the strips toward the top.

3. Chain sew 3 1/4" same light print strips to the units, as shown.

4. Cut the units apart and press the seam allowances toward the last strip added. Stack them with the last strip toward the top.

5. Chain sew 3 1/4" dark print strips to the units, as shown.

6. Cut the units apart and press the seam allowances, as before. Stack them with the last strip added toward the top. *(continued on page 18)*

16

*Civil war reproduction fabrics inspired Kathy Rapley of Overland Park, Kansas, to make **"Log Cabin."** Kathy assembled her blocks in the traditional Barn Raising setting but gave the quilt a unique twist with an original border. The machine quilting was done by Dana Davis of Overland Park, Kansas.*

(continued from page 16)

7. Chain sew 4" same dark print strips to the units, as shown.

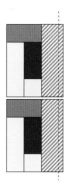

8. Cut the units apart and press.

9. Continue adding strips in the same manner, until the blocks have 3 light and 3 dark strips on each side, as shown.

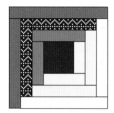

10. Set aside 12 blocks for the outer border.

11. Continue adding strips to the remaining blocks until the blocks have 5 light and 5 dark strips on each side, as shown.

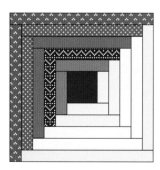

Assembly

1. Referring to the quilt photo on page 17, lay out the blocks in 8 rows of 8. Sew the blocks into rows and join the rows.

2. Sew two 2" x 40" dark red solid strips together, end to end, to make a border. Make 4.

3. Measure the length of the quilt. Trim 2 of the red borders to that measurement. Sew them to opposite sides of the quilt.

4. Measure the width of the quilt, including the borders. Trim the remaining red borders to that measurement. Sew them to the remaining sides of the quilt.

For the outer border:

1. Sew 5 assorted 1 1/4" x 40" dark print strips that were set aside for the border, together along their length, to make a pieced panel. Make 13.

2. Cut seventy-four 7" sections from the pieced panels.

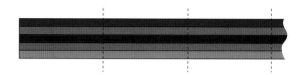

3. Lay out 4 border blocks, eight 7" light print strips, and four 7" dark print strips. Join them, as shown, to make a border unit.

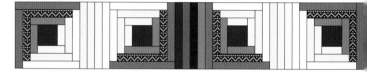

4. Sew 8 sections to each end of the border unit to make a border. Make 2.

5. Referring to the quilt photo, center and sew the borders to opposite sides of the quilt. Start, stop, and backstitch 1/4" from the edge of the quilt top.

6. Lay out 5 sections and one 7" dark print strip and sew them together to make a pieced strip.

7. Sew two 7" light print strips to each end of the pieced strip. Sew 2 border blocks to the pieced strip, as shown, to make a border unit.

8. Sew 8 sections to each end of the border unit to make a border. Make 2.

9. Center and sew the borders to the remaining sides of the quilt, as before.

10. Miter the corners as described in the *General Directions*.

11. Finish the quilt as described in the *General Directions*, using the 2 1/2" x 40" dark red solid strips for the binding.

(continued from page 12)

pieced unit to the bottom keeping the first pieced unit out of the way.

7. Finish sewing the partial seam to complete a block. Make 32.

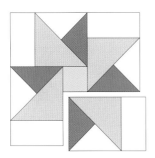

Assembly

1. Referring to the Assembly Diagram lay out the blocks, 4 1/4" x 9 3/4" yellow sashing strips, 4 1/4" off-white squares, small off-white sashing triangles, and the setting and corner triangles.

2. Sew the blocks, sashings, and setting and corner triangles into diagonal rows.

3. Sew the sashings, 4 1/4" off-white squares, and small off-white triangles into diagonal rows.

4. Sew the block rows and sashing rows together.

5. Measure the length of the quilt. Trim the 5" x 94" yellow strips to that measurement. Sew them to the long sides of the quilt.

6. Measure the width of the quilt, including the borders.

Trim the 5" x 85" yellow strips to that measurement. Sew them to the remaining sides of the quilt.

7. Finish the quilt as described in the *General Directions*, using the 2 1/2" x 100" yellow strips for the binding.

Assembly Diagram

Road to Freedom

(continued from page 14)

6. Layer a 3" x 19" dark print strip and a 3" x 19" light print strip, as before. Make 6 pairs. Trim the ends, as shown.

7. Place the light print strips beside the quilt.

8. Referring to the photo, position the trimmed strips around the edges of the quilt so the dark diagonal "bands" in the interior of the quilt will continue into the border.

The strips will overlap at the corners, giving you sufficient length for mitering.

9. Sew the strips together to make the borders. Center and sew the borders to the light print strips.

10. Sew the borders to the quilt. Start and stop stitching 1/4" from each edge and backstitch.

11. Miter the corners according to the *General Directions*.

12. Finish the quilt as described in the *General Directions*, using the 2 1/2" x 40" brown print strips for the binding.

Sunbonnet Sue

Materials

- 36 assorted solid scraps, each at least 3" square, for the shoes
- 72 assorted 1930s-style reproduction prints, each at least 12" square, for the Sunbonnet Sues and sashing
- 3 yards white for the background
- 1 1/2 yards pink print for the border and binding
- 5 1/8 yards backing fabric
- 82" x 94" piece of batting

Cutting

Appliqué pieces (page 29) are full size and do not include a seam allowance. Make a template from each pattern. Trace around the templates on the right side of the fabric and add a 1/8" to 3/16" turn-under allowance when cutting the pieces out. All other dimensions include a 1/4" seam allowance. NOTE: The quilter flipped the pieces for 4 blocks before tracing so the corner block Sues would face the opposite direction.

For each of 36 Sunbonnet Sue blocks:

Select 4 coordinating reproduction prints and one solid for each block.

- Cut 1: A, solid
- Cut 1: B and E, first reproduction print
- Cut 1: C and D, second reproduction print
- Cut 2: 2 1/2" x 8 1/2" strips, third reproduction print
- Cut 2: 2 1/2" x 10 1/2" strips, third reproduction print
- Cut 4: 2 1/2" squares, fourth reproduction print

Also:

- Cut 36: 9" x 11" rectangles, white, for the block backgrounds
- Cut 8: 3 1/2" x 40" strips, pink print, for the border
- Cut 9: 2 1/2" x 40" strips, pink print, for the binding

Directions

For each block:

1. Pin the appliqué pieces for one block to a 9" x 11" white rectangle.

2. Appliqué the pieces to the rectangle in alphabetical order, using the tip of your needle to turn under the allowance as you sew. There is no need to turn under the allowance or to sew pieces where they will be overlapped by other appliqués.

3. Trim the rectangle to 8 1/2" x 10 1/2", centering the Sunbonnet Sue.

4. Sew two 2 1/2" x 10 1/2" print strips to the sides of the block.

5. Sew 2 1/2" print squares to each end of a 2 1/2" x 8 1/2" print strip to make a pieced strip. Make 2.

6. Sew the pieced strips to the top and bottom of the block.

Assembly

1. Referring to the quilt photo, lay out the blocks in 6 rows of 6.

2. Sew the blocks into rows and join the rows.

3. Sew two 3 1/2" x 40" pink print strips together, end to end, to make a pieced border. Make 4.

4. Measure the length of the quilt. Trim 2 pieced borders to that measurement. Stitch them to the sides of the quilt.

5. Measure the width of the quilt, including the borders. Trim the remaining pieced borders to that measurement and stitch them to the top and bottom of the quilt.

6. Finish the quilt as described in the *General Directions*, using the 2 1/2" x 40" pink print strips for the binding.

Ruth Muldoon of Gladstone, Missouri, just loves 1930s-style reproduction prints and accumulated so many that making **"Sunbonnet Sue"** *was a logical choice. For this attractive quilt, she also framed each of the 36 blocks in reproduction print sashings and cornerstones. Ruth credits Eleanor Burn's book,* Sunbonnet Sue Visits Quilt in a Day *(Quilt in a Day, Inc., 1992) for her sashing inspiration.*

21

Chimney Sweep

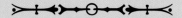

Materials

- 6 1/4 yards tan print
- Assorted red prints, totaling at least 1 5/8 yards
- Assorted brown prints, totaling at least 3 yards
- 8 yards backing fabric
- 91" x 102" piece of batting

Cutting

Dimensions include a 1/4" seam allowance. Cut the lengthwise tan print strips, before cutting other pieces from that fabric.

For each of 72 blocks:
- Cut 1: 2 5/8" x 11" strip, red print
- Cut 1: 2 5/8" x 11" strip, brown print
- Cut 4: 2 5/8" squares, same brown print

Also:
- Cut 8: 2 5/8" x 90" lengthwise strips, tan print
- Cut 5: 2 1/2" x 90" lengthwise strips, tan print, for the binding
- Cut 72: 2 5/8" squares, tan print
- Cut 144: 4 1/4" squares, tan print, then cut them in quarters diagonally to yield 576 large triangles
- Cut 144: 2 3/8" squares, tan print, then cut them in half diagonally to yield 288 small triangles
- Cut 63: 2 5/8" x 9 1/2" strips, tan print

Directions

For each block:

1. Stitch a 2 5/8" x 11" red print strip to a 2 5/8" x 11" brown print strip along their length.

2. Cut four 2 5/8" sections from the pieced strip.

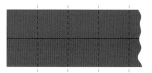

3. Join 2 sections, a 2 5/8" tan print square, and 2 small tan print triangles, as shown.

4. Join a section, a 2 5/8" matching brown print square, and 2 large tan print triangles, as shown. Make 2.

5. Stitch 2 large tan print triangles a 2 5/8" matching brown print square. Stitch a small tan print triangle to the top, as shown. Make 2.

6. Lay out all of the units and join them to complete a Chimney Sweep block. Make 72.

7. Referring to the quilt photo, lay out the blocks in 9 horizontal rows of 8, with 2 5/8" x 9 1/2" tan print strips between the blocks. Stitch the blocks and strips into rows.

8. Measure a row. Trim the 2 5/8" x 90" tan print strips to that measurement.

9. Lay out the rows alternately with the trimmed strips. Join the rows and strips.

10. Finish the quilt as described in the *General Directions*, using the 2 1/2" x 90" tan print strips for the binding.

22

"Chimney Sweep," *made by Judy Forsey of Lockport, New York, looks like an antique, but it isn't. Judy combined a traditional block with reproduction fabrics for a timeless old-fashioned look.*

From Past to Present

©2004 Denice Lipscomb

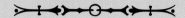

Materials

- **5 1/2 yards background fabric**
- **3 yards red**
- **2 1/2 yards green**
- **1/2 yard yellow**
- **7 1/4 yards backing fabric**
- **85" square of batting**

Cutting

The appliqué pieces (page 30) are full size and do not include a seam allowance. Make a template from each pattern. Trace around the templates on the right side of the fabric and add a 1/8" to 3/16" turn-under allowance as you cut the pieces out. All other dimensions include a 1/4" seam allowance. Cut all strips on the lengthwise grain before cutting other pieces from the same fabric.

From the background fabric:
- Cut 4: 26" squares
- Cut 8: 14" x 26" rectangles
- Cut 4: 14" squares

From the red:
- Cut 5: 2 1/2" x 72" strips, for the binding
- Cut 24: 1 1/2" x 40" strips
- Cut 1: 1 1/2" x 29" strip
- Cut 2: 1 1/2" x 15" strips
- Cut 32: pomegranates
- Cut 4: hearts

From the green:
- Cut 12: 1 1/2" x 40" strips
- Cut 2: 1 1/2" x 29" strips
- Cut 1: 1 1/2" x 15" strip
- Cut 16: stems
- Cut 64: large leaves

- Cut 64: small leaves

From the yellow:
- Cut 32: pomegranate centers

Directions

For the blocks:

1. Fold a 26" background square in quarters and lightly press the folds.

2. Using the creases as guidelines and referring to the photo, arrange the appropriate pieces on the square.

3. Appliqué the pieces to the square. Press the block on the wrong side then trim it to 24 1/2", keeping the appliqué design centered. Make 4 blocks.

4. Appliqué the appropriate pieces to a 14" x 26" rectangle. Keep the V part of the stem 3/4" from the edge of the rectangle.

5. Press the block and trim it to 12 1/2" x 24 1/2", keeping the design centered. Allow a generous 1/4" seam allowance on the V side of the block.

6. Appliqué a heart to each 14" background square. Press the blocks and trim them to 12 1/2" square.

For the sashing:

1. Sew two 1 1/2" x 40" red strips to a 1 1/2" x 40" green strip. Make 12. Press the seam allowances toward the green.

2. Cut one 24 1/2" length and one 12 1/2" length from each pieced strip. Set them aside.

3. Sew two 1 1/2" x 29" green strips to a 1 1/2" x 29" red strip. Press the seam allowances toward the green.

(continued on page 28)

"From Past to Present" *was copied from a 19th century wedding quilt Denice Lipscomb found that was serving as batting inside a newer quilt. The heart quilting designs on the original inspired Denice to appliqué hearts in the corners.*

©2004 Denice Lipscomb

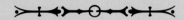

Materials

- 4 yards red print
- 6 1/2 yards light print
- 2 1/2 yards dark stripe
  for the border and binding
- 8 1/4 yards backing fabric
- 86" x 97" piece of batting

Cutting

Dimensions include a 1/4" seam allowance. Cut all strips on the lengthwise grain before cutting other pieces from the same fabric.

From the red print:
- Cut 50: 1 1/2" x 44" strips, then cut twenty-eight 1 1/2" squares from each of 12 strips for a total of 336. Cut seventeen 1 1/2" x 2 1/2" rectangles from each of 20 strips for a total of 340. You will use 336.
- Cut 12: 2 1/2" x 44" strips
- Cut 42: 2 1/2" squares

From the light print:
- Cut 2: 1 1/2" x 81" strips
- Cut 2: 1 1/2" x 70" strips
- Cut 30: 8 1/2" squares
- Cut 6: 12 5/8" squares, then cut them in quarters diagonally to yield 24 setting triangles. You will use 22.
- Cut 2: 6 5/8" squares, then cut them in half diagonally to yield 4 corner triangles
- Cut 44: 1 1/2" x 44" strips, then cut twenty-eight 1 1/2" squares from each of 12 strips for a total of 336. Cut seventeen 1 1/2" x 2 1/2" rectangles from each of 20 strips for a total of 340. You will use 336.
- Cut 12: 2 1/2" x 44" strips

From the dark stripe fabric:
- Cut 4: 6 1/2" x 84" strips, for the border
- Cut 5: 2 1/2" x 75" strips, for the binding

Directions

For the blocks:

1. Sew a 1 1/2" x 44" red print strip to a 2 1/2" x 44" light print strip. Make 12. Press the seam allowances toward the red print.

2. Cut twenty-eight 1 1/2" sections from each pieced strip for a total of 336.

3. Sew two 1 1/2" x 44" light print strips to a 1 1/2" x 44" red print strip. Make 6. Press toward the red.

4. Cut twenty-eight 1 1/2" sections from each pieced strip for a total of 168.

5. Lay out 2 units from the first group and one from the second group. Join them to make a corner unit. Make 168.

6. Place a 1 1/2" red print square on a 1 1/2" x 2 1/2" light print rectangle. Sew from corner to corner, as shown. NOTE: *If you prefer, draw a line on the square before stitching.*

7. Press the square toward the corner, aligning the edges. Trim the seam allowance to 1/4".

8. Sew a red print square to the opposite end of the rectangle. Press and trim to complete a Flying Geese unit. Make 168.

9. In the same manner, make 168 Flying Geese units using light print squares and red print rectangles.

(continued on page 28)

*Denice Lipscomb named **"For Hannah"** after her third great-grandmother. This quilt was part of the Texas Traditonal Treasures exhibit at the Houston Quilt Festival. To see more of Denice's original patterns, visit www.commonthreadsquilting.com.*

For Hannah

(continued from page 26)

10. Lay out a red print rectangle and one Flying Geese unit from the first group and one from the second. Join them to make a side unit. Make 168.

11. Lay out 4 corner units, 4 side units, and a 2 1/2" red print square. Sew them into rows and join the rows to make a block. Make 42.

Assembly

1. Lay out the blocks, the 8 1/2" light print squares, and the setting and corner triangles.

2. Sew the blocks, squares, and triangles into diagonal rows. Join the rows.

3. Measure the length of the quilt. Trim the 1 1/2" x 81" light print strips to that measurement. Sew them to the sides of the quilt.

4. Measure the width of the quilt, including the borders. Trim the 1 1/2" x 70" light print strips to that measurement.

Sew them to the top and bottom of the quilt.

5. In the same manner, trim 2 of the 6 1/2" x 84" dark stripe strips to fit the quilt's length. Sew them to the sides of the quilt.

6. Trim the remaining 6 1/2" x 84" dark stripe strips to fit the quilt's width and sew them to the top and bottom of the quilt.

7. Finish the quilt as described in the *General Directions*, using the 2 1/2" x 75" dark stripe strips for the binding.

Assembly Diagram

From Past to Present

(continued from page 24)

4. Cut eighteen 1 1/2" sections from the pieced strip.

5. Sew two 1 1/2" x 15" red strips to a 1 1/2" x 15" green strip. Press toward the green.

6. Cut nine 1 1/2" sections from the pieced strip.

7. Lay out 2 sections from the first group and one from

the second. Sew them together to make a Nine Patch cornerstone. Make 9.

Assembly

1. Referring to the photo, lay out the blocks, sashing strips, and cornerstones in horizontal rows.

2. Sew the pieces into rows and join the rows.

3. Finish the quilt as described in the *General Directions*, using the 2 1/2" x 72" red strips for the binding.

Full-Size Appliqué Patterns for Sunbonnet Sue

(pattern begins on page 20)

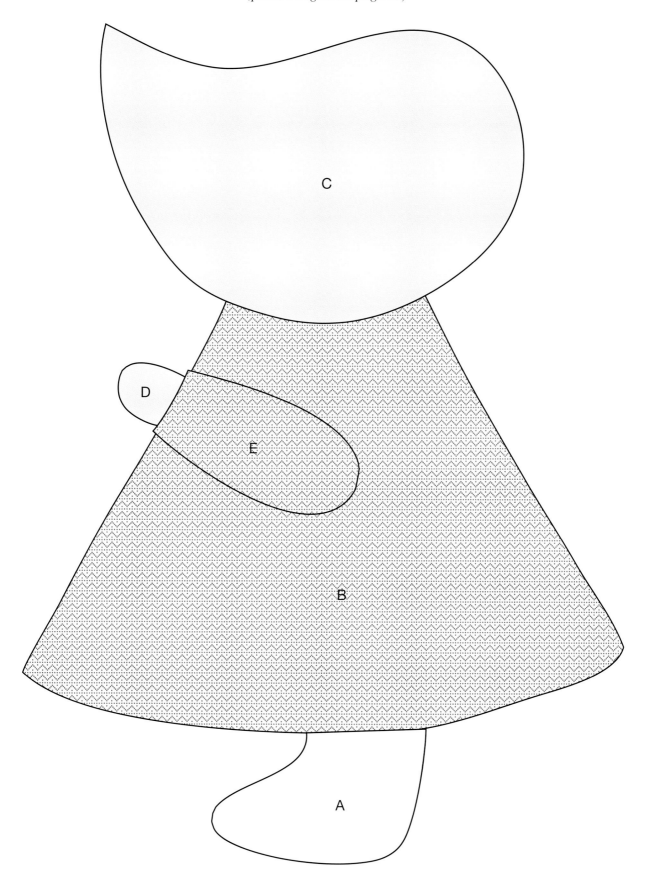

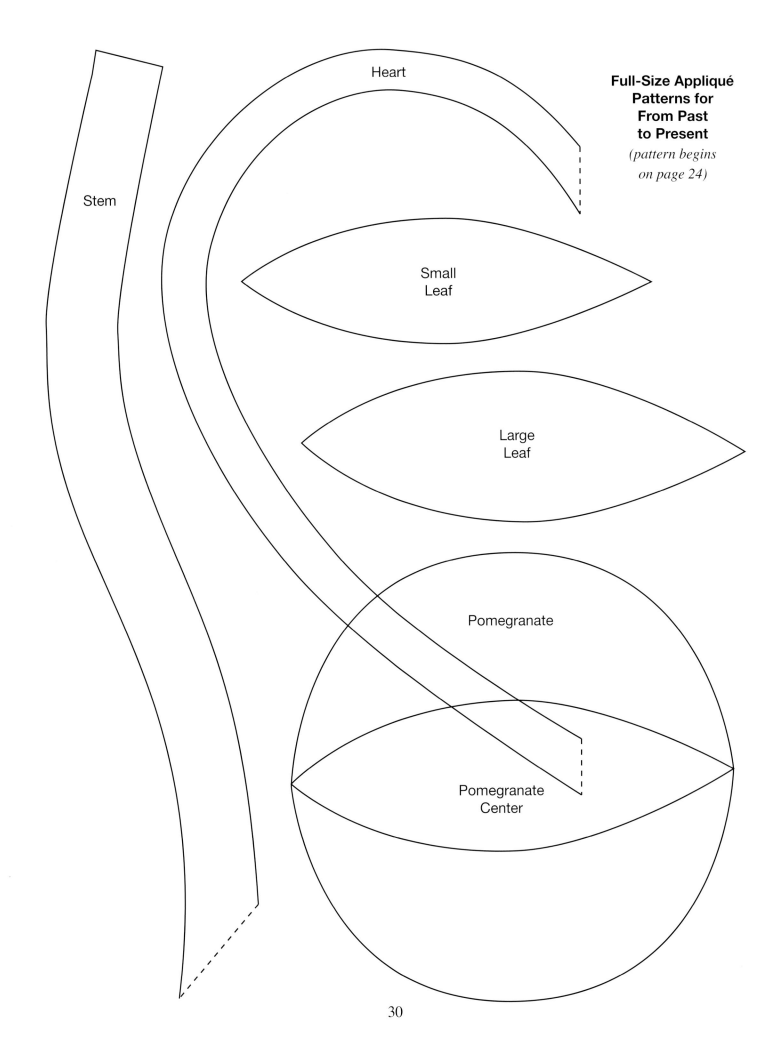

Heart

Stem

**Full-Size Appliqué
Patterns for
From Past
to Present**

*(pattern begins
on page 24)*

Small
Leaf

Large
Leaf

Pomegranate

Pomegranate
Center

General Directions

About the patterns

Read through the pattern directions before cutting fabric. Yardage requirements are based on fabric with a useable width of 40". Pattern directions are given in step-by-step order. If you are sending your quilt to a professional machine quilter, consult the quilter regarding the necessary batting and backing size for your quilt.

Fabrics

We suggest using 100% cotton. Wash fabric in warm water with mild detergent. Do not use fabric softener. Dry fabric on a warm-to-hot setting. Press with a hot dry iron to remove any wrinkles.

Templates

Template patterns are full size and unless otherwise noted, include a 1/4" seam allowance. The solid line is the cutting line; the dashed line is the stitching line. Templates for hand piecing do not include a seam allowance.

Piecing

For machine piecing, sew 12 stitches per inch, exactly 1/4" from the edge of the fabric. To make accurate piecing easier, mark the throat plate with a piece of tape 1/4" to the right of the point where the needle pierces the fabric.

Appliqué

Appliqué pieces can be stitched by hand or machine. To hand appliqué, baste or pin the pieces to the background in stitching order. Turn the edges under with your needle as you appliqué the pieces in place. Do not turn under or stitch edges that will be overlapped by other pieces. Finish the edges of fusible appliqué pieces with a blanket stitch made either by hand or machine.

To machine appliqué, baste pieces in place close to the edges. Then stitch over the basting with a short, wide satin stitch using a piece of tear-away stabilizer under the background fabric. You can also turn the edges of appliqué pieces under as for needleturn appliqué, and stitch them in place with a blind-hem stitch.

Pressing

Press with a dry iron. Press seam allowances toward the darker of the two pieces whenever possible. Otherwise, trim away 1/16" from the darker seam allowance to prevent it from shadowing through. Press abutting seams in opposite directions. Press all blocks, sashings, and borders before assembling the quilt top.

Mitered Borders

Measure the length of the quilt top and add 2 times the border width plus 2". Cut border strips this measurement. Match the center of the quilt top with the center of the border strip and pin to the corners. Stitch—beginning, ending, and backstitching each seamline 1/4" from the edge of the quilt top. After all borders have been attached, miter one corner at a time. With the quilt top right side down, lay one border over the other. Draw a straight line at a 45° angle from the inner to the outer corners.

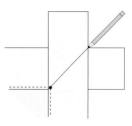

Reverse the position of the borders and mark another corner-to-corner line. With the borders right sides together and the marked seamlines carefully matched, stitch from the inner to the outer corner, backstitching at each end. Open the mitered seam to make sure it lies flat, then trim excess fabric and press.

FINISHING YOUR QUILT
Binding

Cut the binding strips with the grain for straight-edge quilts. Binding for quilts with curved edges must be cut on the bias. To make 1/2" finished binding, cut 2 1/2"-wide strips. Sew strips together with diagonal seams; trim and press seam allowance open.

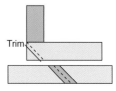

Trim

Fold the strip in half lengthwise, wrong side in, and press. Position the strip on the right side of the quilt top, aligning the raw edges of the binding with the edge of the quilt top. Leaving 6" of the binding strip free and beginning a few inches from one corner, stitch the binding to the quilt with a 1/4" seam allowance measuring from the raw edge of the quilt top. When you reach a corner, stop stitching 1/4" from the edge of the quilt top and backstitch. Clip the threads and remove the quilt from the machine. Fold the binding up and away from the quilt, forming a 45° angle, as shown.

Keeping the angled fold secure, fold the binding back down. This fold should be even with the edge of the quilt top. Begin stitching at the fold.

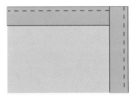

Continue stitching around the quilt in this manner to within 6" of the starting point. To finish, fold both strips back along the edge of the quilt so that the folded edges meet about 3" from both lines of the stitching and the binding lies flat on the quilt. Finger press to crease the folds. Measure the width of the folded binding. Cut the strips that distance beyond the folds. (In this case 1 1/4" beyond the folds.)

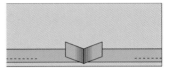

Open both strips and place the ends at right angles to each other, right sides together. Fold the bulk of the quilt out of your way. Join the strips with a diagonal seam as shown.

Trim the seam allowance to 1/4" and press it open. Refold the strip wrong side in. Place the binding flat against the quilt, and finish stitching it to the quilt. Trim excess batting and backing so that the binding edge will be filled with batting when you fold the binding to the back of the quilt. Blindstitch the binding to the back, covering the seamline.

Remove visible markings. Make a label that includes your name, the date the quilt was completed, and any other pertinent information, and stitch it to the back of your quilt.